Sew
Advent
Calendars

First published in 2017

Search Press Limited
Wellwood, North Farm Road,
Tunbridge Wells, Kent TN2 3DR

Photographs by Garie Hind

ISBN: 978-1-78221-488-5

Suppliers
For details of suppliers, please visit the
Search Press website: www.searchpress.com

For further inspiration, visit Debbie's website:
www.debbieshore.tv

Printed in China by 1010 Printing International Ltd

Sew
Advent
Calendars

Debbie Shore

Count down to Christmas with 20 stylish designs to fill with festive treats

SEARCH PRESS

Contents

Quick Cones,
page 56

Calendar Cubes,
page 60

Advent Bunting,
page 62

Canine Calendar,
page 88

Hanging Mittens,
page 92

Introduction

For adults and children alike, the build-up to Christmas is such a special time of the year. I look forward to the change in the weather, shopping for gifts and planning meals and get-togethers with family and friends. Many of us will buy or make advent calendars – particularly if we have children – to count down the days and create excitement leading up to Christmas day. I remember my children's excitement when the calendars appeared on the kitchen door – it was the only time of year they were allowed a (very small!) chocolate before breakfast!

But what does advent actually mean? The word itself is Latin for 'coming', and marks the start of the festive season, beginning four Sundays before Christmas. Advent calendars, however, don't typically follow this period of time; instead, they tend to begin on December 1st, building up to December 25th, Christmas day. Advent calendars can count either the weeks or days leading up to Christmas. Some calendars will simply highlight how many days or weeks remain, some will contain small gifts. So, you'll find some advent calendars with four numbers only, some with up to twenty-four days and some including the 25th. The choice is yours! In this book we're going to create calendars that you'll want to bring out year after year, for all the family – old and young alike. Some fun, some elegant, with or without gifts, counting days or weeks. I have a few ideas for treats, and different ways of numbering the projects to help you create your own personal calendars (see pages 15–17). I'm sure you'll enjoy making them as much as I have! Use a 5mm (¼in) seam allowance, unless otherwise stated, and 100% cotton fabric.

Debbie

Sewing essentials

FABRICS

I like to use 100% cotton fabric and wool/viscose felt. The colours and prints you choose can make your projects fit with any decor, from traditional Christmas reds and greens to contemporary silvers and lilacs. Change the fabrics in any of my designs to create the look and feel you want, for adults or for children.

WADDING/BATTING AND STABILISER

There are many different weights and fibre contents of wadding/batting, and it can be man-made or natural, fusible or sew-in. For my advent calendars I've used a cotton and polyester blend for softer projects such as the Four-week Calendar (see pages 70–73), and a single-sided fusible fleece for a more rigid feel to the hanging calendars. A foam stabiliser will give a firmer finish if you prefer; the best way to decide is to visit a fabric store and have a feel of the different types to see which one will best suit your project.

SEWING MACHINE

For the projects in this book you won't need a top-of-the-range machine (as much as you'd like one!) but a range of stitches and feet are always useful. You'll need to be able to drop the feed dogs and use a darning foot for free-motion embroidery, and a walking foot is helpful if you're sewing through layers of fabric.

Free-motion embroidery foot

Think of your needle and thread as a pen and ink, but instead of moving the pen over the paper, you move the fabric under the needle to create your own unique designs. There are two things you'll need for your sewing machine: a drop feed dog facility and a free-motion or darning foot (see below). This foot 'hops' across the fabric, and allows you to see where you're stitching. It's a good idea to practise first on a piece of fabric you're not too precious about!

Walking foot

This foot (see right) helps to feed your fabric through the machine from the top, as the feed dogs work from the bottom, allowing layers of fabric or different weights of fabric to pass under the needle more smoothly.

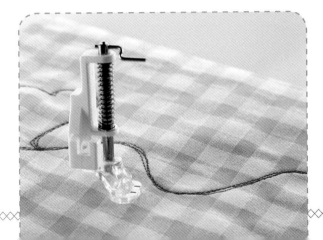

ROTARY CUTTER, RULER AND MAT

Invest in these: you'll save time, and they will help you measure and cut accurately. The most popular size rotary cutter is 45mm (1¾in); go for the largest mat and ruler you have space for.

MARKING TOOLS

Air-erasable pens deliver ink that disappears after a few hours; water-erasable ink goes away when wet. I tend to use heat-erasable ink pens that disappear due to either friction or heat from the iron. Fabric pencils are useful and are available in both light and dark colours so they stand out against any fabric. Chalk is an option but can be difficult to make an accurate mark with.

ADHESIVES

A repositionable fabric spray for appliqué, permanent fabric glue spray that adheres when ironed, and a strong wet glue are my essentials. A dot of wet glue will hold buttons in place and sprays will make wadding/ batting fusible. For quick, strong adhesion you can't beat a glue gun, but do be careful to keep your fingers away from the wet glue – it really does get hot!

THREADS

Keep as many colours in stock as you can, but make sure they are all of good quality – your projects will last longer and your sewing machine will appreciate them!

SCISSORS

Dressmaking shears – used just for fabrics – are a must-have, along with a small pair of scissors to snip threads. Pinking shears will help to stop your fabric from fraying and create a zigzag effect on felt.

Sewing know-how

Machine stitches

Straight stitch
Straight stitch is used to join fabric together, hem items or add a topstitch.

Zigzag stitch
Zigzag stitch is used around hems to help stop the fabric fraying, and as decoration.

Back-tacking
At the start and end of each row of machine sewing, reverse a few stitches to stop the stitches coming undone. This is particularly important when sewing the pockets on your calendars as the stitches will be under strain when the pockets are filled with treats! Some machines have a locking stitch that sews three or four stitches close together – this does the same job.

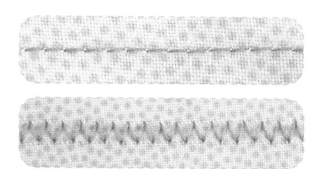

Hand stitches

I used only basic hand embroidery stitches to decorate my Hanging Mittens bunting (see pages 92–94). If you're not too confident, draw a guideline with an erasable ink pen first. Use blanket stitch to edge fabrics such as felt to give a decorative finish; a decorative chain stitch is created by looping the thread around the needle as you sew; a simple star stitch – made of three crossing straight stitches – looks like a little snowflake!

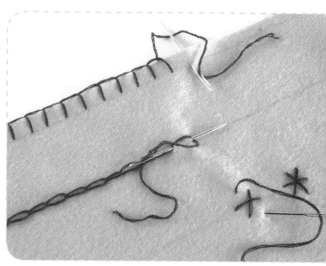

Cutting into a seam

When sewing a curve, the seam will sit flatter if you make little snips into the seam allowance before turning through. Pinking shears also do the job very well.

Snipping off corners

To help the corners of your calendars and pockets form a sharp square, cut across the corners of the fabric before turning to reduce the bulk of fabric. Be careful not to snip through the stitches!

Fussy cutting

This is the term used for cutting a specific area of your fabric, for instance for the snowman's pockets (see pages 52–55).

Making bias binding

Although bias strips (also referred to as bias binding and bias tape) can be bought in many colours and sizes, I like to make my own, as this is cost-effective and means I can coordinate it with my fabrics.

Bias binding is a strip of fabric cut on the diagonal, at a 45° angle, which allows a little 'give' so that the fabric stretches around curves without puckering. To cut your fabric accurately you will need a rotary cutter, rectangular ruler and cutting mat.

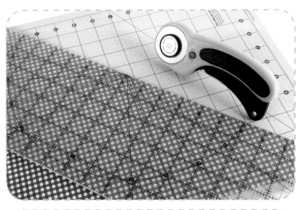

1 Lay your fabric squarely on the cutting mat, and place the 45° mark on your ruler on the straight edge of the fabric. Cut along the ruler. Use the straight side of the ruler to measure the width you need. For 2.5cm (1in) bias binding, you need to cut 5cm (2in) of fabric. As you are cutting the strips, the fabric will stretch, so fold it in half diagonally and cut through two, three or four layers at a time.

2 To join the strips, lay two pieces right sides together, overlapping at right angles. Draw a diagonal line from one corner to the other, as in the photograph. Pin, then sew along this line. Trim the raw edge back to around 3mm (1/8in) and press the seam open.

3 To make bias binding, you need to fold both of the long edges of the tape into the centre and press. The easiest way to do this is to use either a bias binding machine or a small bias tape maker. As you pull the strip through this, it folds it in two – press with your iron to fix the folds. If you don't have a tape maker, carefully fold both long edges to the centre of the fabric strip and press. Be careful not to get your fingers too close to the iron!

Applying bias binding

And here's how to apply your bias binding. A neat, mitred corner really gives a professional finish to a project, and it's not difficult when you know how...

1 Open out the bias tape and pin right sides together with the edge of your project. Fold over the first end of the binding. Sew along the crease line but stop 1cm (½in) from the corner and back-tack to stop the stitches coming undone.

2 Take the tape along the second side, making a triangular pleat in the corner. Fold the pleat away from your stitch line, pin in place, and sew along the second side, again stopping 1cm (½in) from the end.

3 Continue in the same way around the next three corners. When you're back to where you started, overlap the ends of the tape by about 5mm (¼in).

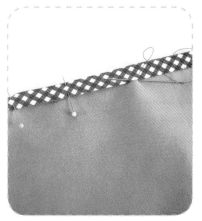

4 Fold the tape over to the back, tucking the folded edge under, and you should see neat mitres forming: mirror the same mitres on the reverse. You might need to use fabric clips to hold the edges together as the fabric will now be quite thick. Sew the bias tape in place by hand with a slip stitch, making sure your machine stitch line is covered by the tape.

5 When you're finished you'll have really neat, square corners both from the front of your work and from the back!

Adding treats

Advent calendars don't always include treats, but here
are a few ideas for if you'd like to fill yours with small gifts.

- Sweets/candies or chocolates
- Crayons and small craft items
- Jewellery
- Toy cars
- Hair clips and hair ties
- Nail varnish/polish
- Miniature drinks
- Christmas decorations

- Tealight candles
- Home-made biscuits/cookies
- Speciality tea bags
- Messages, promises and tasks,
for instance: 'today I will cook all the
meals' or 'you can have the TV remote
all day today!'

Counting down

There are many ways of adding numbers to your advent calendar projects. You could draw and cut out your own but this can be time-consuming – why not consider some of these quicker and easier options?

FELT NUMBERS

The easiest option is to buy pre-cut felt numbers. They are available in a wide range of sizes and colours, and some are fusible, meaning you can simply iron them in place onto your fabric.

STAMPING

Stamping your numbers is another fun option; use an ink that is suitable for fabric and run an iron over the numbers to set the ink.

DIE-CUT NUMBERS

If you have a die-cutting machine, using number dies is a quick way of accurately cutting your numbers. Felt is a good choice of fabric as it won't fray; try fusing a bonding adhesive sheet to the back.

USING TEMPLATES

Plastic templates are perfect for larger numbers: simply draw around them onto your fabric and cut out. You could either hand sew, machine sew or free-motion embroider them in place.

BUTTONS

Or why not simply sew on some lovely number buttons?

WOODEN NUMBERS

Laser-cut wooden numbers will give a rustic look to your calendar, and can easily be painted if you prefer them in a different colour.

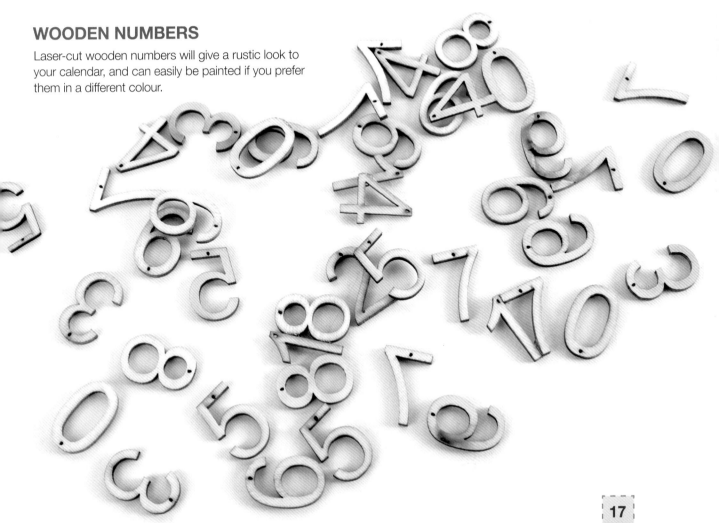

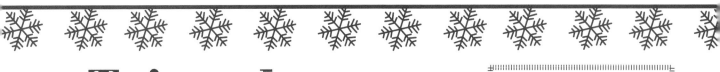

Triangle Pockets

These triangular pockets give a patchwork look to this eye-catching calendar, adding a little twist to the traditional style. This fun, playful fabric is perfect for little kids (and grown-up big kids!) but you could change it for muted colours for a very different feel.

Finished size

40.5 x 56cm (16 x 22in)

What you need

Two pieces of backing fabric measuring 42 x 56cm (16½ x 22in)

42 x 56cm (16½ x 22in) fusible fleece

23cm (¼yd) pocket fabric

2.5m (8¼ft) of 2.5cm (1in) wide bias binding

Felt numbers, 1–25

Fabric glue

Four pincer clips with rings

45.75cm (17¼in) dowelling rail

1 Cut fifty 7.5cm (3in) squares from the pocket fabric. Sew in pairs right sides together, leaving a small turning gap in one side. Snip across the corners.

2 Turn right side out and press. With the turning gap at the bottom, fold over the top point by 4cm (1½in) and press. Pop a little glue under each flap.

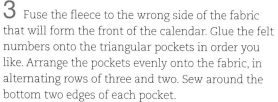

3 Fuse the fleece to the wrong side of the fabric that will form the front of the calendar. Glue the felt numbers onto the triangular pockets in order you like. Arrange the pockets evenly onto the fabric, in alternating rows of three and two. Sew around the bottom two edges of each pocket.

4 Place this panel wrong sides together with the fabric that will form the back of the calendar, pin together, then apply bias binding all the way round, mitring the corners and overlapping the ends to make neat (see page 14).

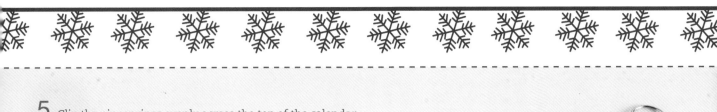

5 Clip the pincer rings evenly across the top of the calendar.

6 Attach the calendar to the dowelling rail. If you don't have a handy hanger like mine, tie a length of ribbon at each end of the rail and hang it from a hook.

Tip
Instead of pincer clips you could use small bulldog clips or sew ribbon ties to the top.

12 Days of Christmas

Count down the 12 days to Christmas with a treat under each one of these fun cones! Make them in any size you like, and embellish them with buttons, sequins, ribbon or ric rac braid for a fun Christmas display along a mantelpiece.

Finished size

Small: 10cm (4in) tall
Large: 30.5cm (12in)

What you need

91.5cm (36in) square foam stabiliser

183cm (2yd) bright coloured fabric – use a mixture of patterns and prints

Buttons, beads and sequins: as many as you'd like to add!

Numbers 1–12: I used a different style of number on each cone

Free-motion embroidery foot for your sewing machine

Card, pen and a ruler with a 60º angle to make templates: I made seven different sizes

Erasable ink pen

Repositionable spray adhesive

Star template, page 96

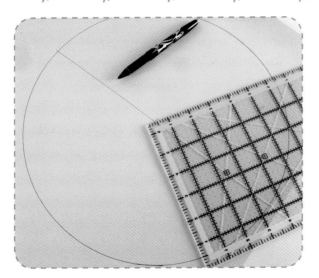

1 Make a template for your cones by drawing a circle on a piece of card; the radius of the circle will be the height of your cone, minus seam allowances. Mark the centre of the circle and draw a line straight across the middle. Use the 60° angle on your ruler to divide the circle into thirds.

2 Cut out one third of the circle and use this as your cone template.

3 Cut a piece of foam stabiliser using your template.

4 Cut two pieces of fabric 1cm (½in) larger all the way round than your foam piece. Use a little spray adhesive to adhere the foam to the wrong side of one piece of fabric.

5 Draw a quilting design onto the foam-backed fabric using an erasable ink pen, either free hand or using the star template on page 96. If you're using a printed fabric, you could simply echo the design.

6 Using your sewing machine, free-motion embroider over the lines. If you don't have this facility, use a straight stitch or hand sew a running stitch.

7 Notice how the stitches sink into the foam, giving a three-dimensional effect to the fabric.

8 Add the number to the centre of the cone, then embellish all around it with beads or buttons.

9 Take the second piece of fabric and place right sides together with the first. Sew around the curve – try not to sew through the foam stabiliser.

10 Open out the fabric and sew the straight sides together, right sides facing – leave a turning gap in the lining of about 7.5cm (3in).

11 Turn right side out, then sew the lining closed. Push the lining inside the cone. Pop a couple of hand stitches through all the layers in the point of the cone to hold the lining in place. Topstitch around the base of the cone.

12 Make up another eleven cones in varying sizes and colours; decorate as you wish!

Tip

If you make the cones in red, trimmed with white, you've made Santa hats!

Christmas Cottages

These cute cottages have pockets to hold Christmas treats. The doors and windows are great for using up small scrap pieces of fabric, and you can decorate them as you like to suit your Christmas colour scheme!

Finished size

Each cottage:
6.5 x 13cm (2½ x 5in)

What you need

Four fat eighths of neutral fabrics for the pockets, cut into twenty-five 7.5 x 15.25cm (3 x 6in) pieces

Two fat quarters of patterned fabric for the roofs, cut into fifty 7.5 x 11.5cm (3 x 4½in) pieces

Twenty-five pieces of plain fabric for the doors, each measuring 2.5 x 4cm (1 x 1½in)

Free-motion embroidery foot

Twenty-five 2cm (¾in) squares of fabric for the windows

Twenty-five strips of ribbon or lace trim, each measuring 9cm (3½in) in length

127cm (50in) of narrow ribbon or cord for hanging, cut into 5cm (2in) lengths

Number stamps and fabric ink

Optional decorations: small buttons for door handles, felt leaves and felt triangular Christmas trees; I decorated a few cottages with flowers cut out from a printed fabric.

1 Take a neutral piece of fabric and fold in half to crease the centre line.

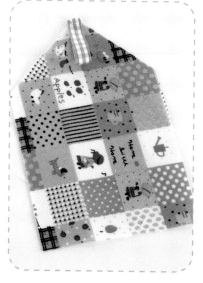

2 Embellish the bottom half of the neutral fabric with ribbon trim, a 'door' and a 'window'; free-motion embroider these in place. Use a small button as a door handle, a felt triangle for a tree and a bead to decorate the tree. Stamp a number on the door. Fold this section back in half again, wrong sides together.

3 On two of the patterned roof pieces, mark 4cm (1½in) down on each side. Mark and then cut from these points to the centre top, to make a 'house' shape. Fold a 5cm (2in) piece of ribbon in half and tack/baste facing inwards to the point of one of the roof pieces.

4 Sew this roof piece right sides together to the bottom of the folded, embellished pocket piece.

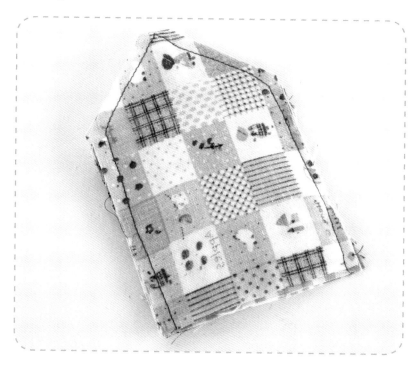

5 Place a second 'roof' piece of fabric over this section so that the embellished pocket is sandwiched in between the two roofs. Sew along either side and the top, leaving the bottom edge open. Snip across the top point.

6 Turn right side out. Sew the opening closed.

7 Turn again through the pocket and press.

8 Repeat for the other twenty-four cottages! Hang them along a length of cord to display them.

25 Steps to Christmas

A stair banister makes a simple backdrop for these advent parcels. If you don't have stairs, try hanging them from a length of ribbon or cord instead. The pouches can be made in any size you like, and are simply closed with a clothes peg/pin.

Finished size

Each pouch: 11.5 x 10cm (4½ x 4in)

What you need

Fifty 13cm (5in) squares of fabric in Christmas prints

Twenty-five clothes pegs/pins

Numbers 1–25: I used 10cm (4in) plastic templates

One fat quarter of plain fabric

Double-sided iron-on adhesive sheets

Approximately 51cm (20in) of ribbon in various colours

Free-motion embroidery foot

1 I chose coordinating red and grey Christmas fabrics for my fabric squares.

2 Fuse the adhesive sheet to the wrong side of your plain fabric. Draw around the numbers using your templates and cut out enough for 1–25.

3 Peel the backing sheet away from the numbers and iron onto twenty-five of the squares. Free-motion embroider around the shapes (see page 9).

4 Sew one numbered square right sides together with an unnumbered square, leaving the top open. Pinch the two bottom corners so that the side seams meet the base seam, and sew across the corners, 2.5cm (1in) from each point.

5 Trim away the excess fabric at the point. Turn right side out. Fold the top of the bag over twice and topstitch. Repeat with the twenty-four remaining parcels!

Tip

If you don't have clothes pegs/pins, large paper clips or colourful bulldog clips will do the trick!

6 Hand sew a length of ribbon to the centre back of each pouch to hang it up. Pop in your treats and tie to the banister spindles.

Felt Pyramids

These little triangular pockets create a contemporary calendar, and are really easy to make! I made a tree from twigs from my garden – I simply tied them together with string and spray painted them white. I've also added a string of delicate lights on a copper wire.

Finished size

Each pyramid:
5 x 5cm (2 x 2in)

What you need

Twenty-five rectangles of felt measuring 10 x 5cm (4 x 2in) – I used a combination of blue, grey, green and white, with one red for Christmas day

Wooden craft numbers, 1–25

Embroidery thread

1 Take one rectangle of felt and fold it in half. Sew along one side, adjacent to the fold.

2 Squash the opposite side to the seam so that the two corners meet and sew again. You'll create an opening in which to put a small gift.

3 Sew a loop of embroidery thread to the top point for hanging, then sew a wooden number to the opposite end, leaving a length of thread to make the number dangle. Repeat to create the other twenty-four pyramids.

Tip
You'll find numbers 10–25 easier to attach if you glue the two numbers together first.

Twig Pouches

Make these little pouches to fit any size gift you like; tying them to a twig gives a rustic look to this calendar.

Finished size

Large: 11.5 x 13cm
(4½ x 5in)
Small: 7.5 x 9cm (3 x 3½in)

What you need

Three fat quarters of contrasting cotton fabrics

11m (36ft) in total of twine, ribbon or cord, or all three!

30.5cm (12in) square of calico

Number stamps and ink

A twig measuring around 90cm (35½in) in length

1 Cut the calico into twenty-five squares of approximately 2.5cm (1in), but vary the sizes slightly. Fray the edges a little, then stamp a number in the centre of each.

2 For each large pouch, cut two rectangles of fabric measuring 13 x 15.25cm (5 x 6in). For each small pouch, cut two rectangles measuring 9 x 10cm (3½ x 4in). Use pinking shears to trim across the top – a short side – of each piece.

3 Sew a numbered calico square onto the front piece of each pouch, 2.5cm (1in) up from the bottom. Don't worry about the patch being perfectly straight!

4 For each pouch, sew the two pieces right sides together across the bottom short side.

5 With the pieces right sides together, fold the seamed edge up between the two layers by 1cm (½in) and pin in place; this creates the squared bottom.

6 Sew along each side. Turn the pouch right side out.

7 Cut a 46cm (18in) length of cord, measure 20.5cm (8in) from one end and sew this point by hand to one side seam of the pouch, 4cm (1½in) down from the top. Place a small gift inside the pouch, then tie cord around the top to make a bow.

8 When your twenty-five pouches are complete, tie them along the twig at different heights, trimming the excess cord as necessary. Tie a loop of cord to either end of the twig to hang it up.

Lace Pocket Calendar

This is a great way to use up scraps of fabric and odd lengths of ribbon and lace in your stash. Keeping the colour tones quite neutral gives a vintage feel to the calendar, while the randomness of the pockets creates a modern look. I've made the number 25 pocket from red fabric to make it stand out.

1 Take each one of the twenty-five pocket pieces and fold in half, right sides together.

2 Sew around the edges, leaving a turning gap in one side. Snip off the corners.

3 Turn right side out and press.

Finished size

38 x 48.25cm (15 x 19in)

What you need

For the backing:
One piece of hessian/burlap measuring 38 x 48.25cm (15 x 19in)

One piece of fusible wadding/batting measuring 38 x 48.25cm (15 x 19in)

One piece of backing fabric measuring 38 x 48.25cm (15 x 19in)

Three strips of lace 38cm (15in) in length, various widths

178cm (70in) of 2.5cm (1in) wide bias binding

Fabric glue

For the pockets, in assorted complementary prints:
Twelve pieces of fabric measuring 13 x 15.25cm (5 x 6in)

Twelve pieces of fabric measuring 7.5 x 15.25cm (3 x 6in)

One piece of red fabric measuring 13 x 15.25cm (5 x 6in)

Adhesive felt numbers: numbers 1–24 in beige, number 25 in red

Ribbon, lace and buttons to trim

To hang:
48.25cm (19in) of 1cm (½in) wide dowelling

61cm (24in) twine

Two pieces of 1cm (½in) wide ribbon, 13cm (5in) each in length

4 Decorate each pocket with ribbon, lace and buttons. Leave the opening at the bottom so that it will be closed when sewn onto the background fabric.

5 Fuse your wadding/batting to the back of your hessian/burlap piece. Sew the strips of lace to the hessian/burlap, 7.5cm (3in), 18cm (7in) and 44.5cm (17½in) down from the top. Arrange the pockets on top, starting with the top row and overlapping a few – but make sure they don't overlap so far that you can't fit a gift inside! Secure with a little glue on the bottom edges. Leave at least 1cm (½in) free around the edges to accommodate the bias binding.

6 Sew the pockets in place, leaving the top of each open. Now arrange and stick on the numbers – I've left this stage until now so that I can make sure the numbers are all visible.

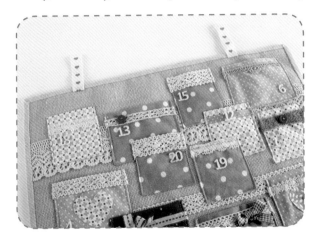

7 Fold the two hanging strips of ribbon in half wrong sides together, and tack/baste facing inwards to the top of the calendar, 7.5cm (3in) from each side. Place the backing fabric wrong sides together to the back. I prefer to machine stitch the bias tape from the front, then hand sew to the back, mitring the corners (see page 14).

8 Ready to add your dowelling and twine and hang up!

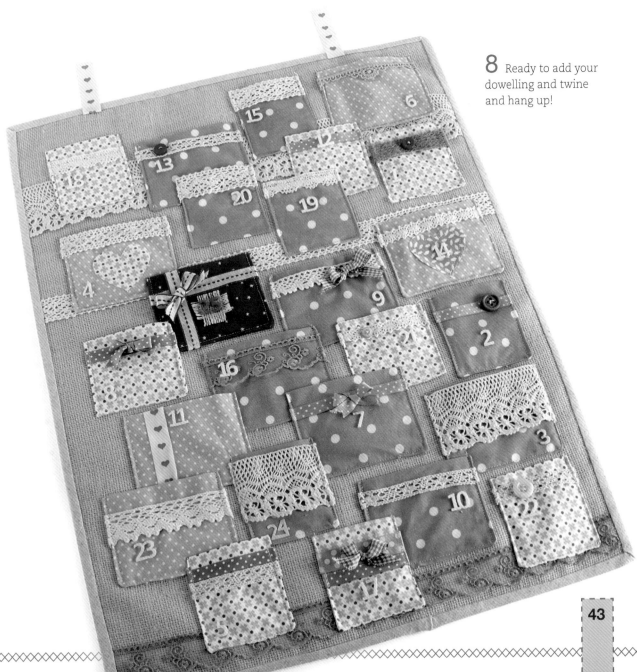

Pleated Pockets

This calendar works particularly well with a striped fabric, which makes it easy to make uniform pleats. It's a simple technique and you can make the pockets any size you like.

Finished size

38 x 44.5cm (15 x 17½in)

What you need

One piece of fabric measuring 109.25 x 40.5cm (43 x 16in)

One piece of backing fabric measuring 48.25 x 40.5cm (19 x 16in)

One piece of wadding/batting measuring 48.25 x 40.5cm (19 x 16in)

15.25cm (6in) square of hessian/burlap

Pre-cut felt numbers, 1–24

Two lengths of ribbon, each measuring 38cm (15in)

Baton to hang, 40.5cm (16in) long

Spray fabric adhesive

Erasable ink pen

A 61cm (24in) ruler

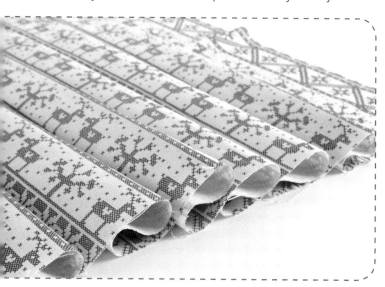

1 Pinch the long strip of fabric to form six pleats. Each pleat should measure about 5cm (2in). I used the pattern on my fabric to gauge the measurement; the sizes of the pockets can vary as long as the pleats are straight.

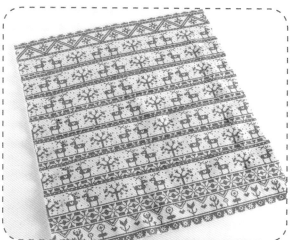

2 Pin the pleats in place and press.

3 Spray the back of the panel with adhesive and adhere to the wadding/batting. You may need to trim this down a little. Draw lines with your erasable ink pen to divide the pockets, 10cm (4in) apart.

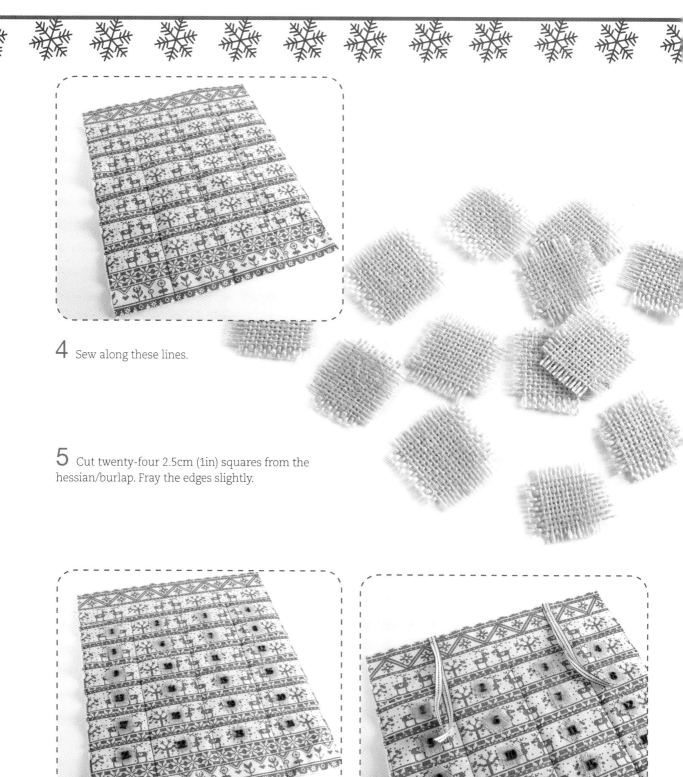

4 Sew along these lines.

5 Cut twenty-four 2.5cm (1in) squares from the hessian/burlap. Fray the edges slightly.

6 Glue a square hessian/burlap piece to the top front of each pocket, then glue the numbers on top.

7 Fold the ribbon pieces in half. Tack/baste the folded end of each, facing inwards, to the top of the calendar, 10cm (4in) from the side.

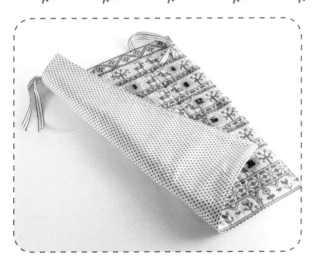

8 Pin the front piece right sides together with the backing fabric; you may need to trim the backing slightly. Sew all the way round, leaving a turning gap of about 10cm (4in) in one side. Turn right side out and press. Topstitch around the edge – this will close the opening.

Tip

I glued the numbers in order here, but you could mix them up so that the lucky recipient has to search for their treat each day!

9 Tie to your baton and fill with treats!

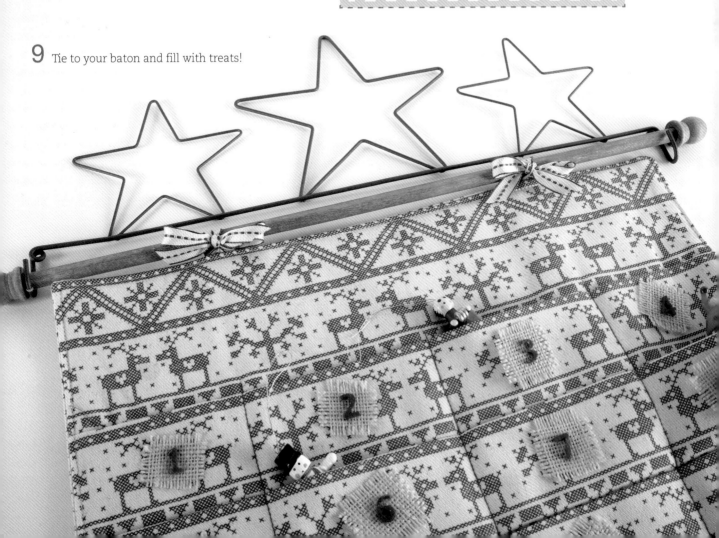

Calendar Girl

Chalk how many sleeps to Santa on your calendar girl's little blackboard, then after Christmas she could show you special dates or gentle reminders!

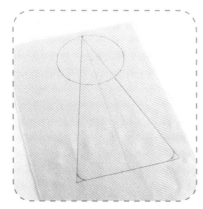

1 To make the doll's head and body, draw a circle using your 15.25cm (6in) circle template. Draw a 38cm (15in) line straight down from the centre top of the circle. Draw another line centrally across the bottom of this line, measuring 20.5cm (8in). Join the three points to form a triangle. Round off the bottom corners.

2 Cut out two head and body shapes.

3 Cut four pieces of fabric for the legs, measuring 6.5 x 28cm (2½ x 11in) and four for the arms, measuring 5.75 x 20.5cm (2¼ x 8in). Round off one end of each piece using your 6.5cm (2½in) circle template.

Finished size

Standing: 61cm (24in) tall

What you need

15.25cm (6in) circle template
6.5cm (2½in) circle template
46cm (½yd) seeded cotton or plain fabric
15.25 x 20.5cm (6 x 8in) fabric for the shoes
102 x 25.5cm (40 x 10in) fabric for the dress
Erasable ink pen
Free-motion embroidery foot
Approximately 250g (9oz) of toy filler
Strong wet fabric glue
Five buttons
76cm (30in) of 1cm (½in) wide ribbon
Knitting yarn for the hair
A 15.25cm (6in) rectangular ruler
Pink blusher
An old CD or DVD
30.5cm (12in) square of blackboard fabric
51cm (20in) of 2.5cm (1in) wide bias binding
Chalk stick

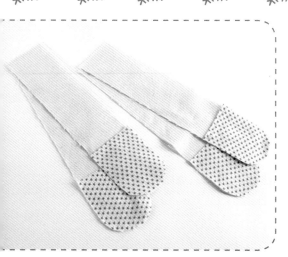  

4 Use the rounded end of the leg as a template to create the shoes: cut four pieces of fabric measuring 9cm (3½in) long. Fold over the straight side by 5mm (¼in) and press. Place these over the ends of the legs and topstitch in place along the folded edge.

5 Using a small stitch, sew the leg and arm pieces right sides together in pairs, leaving the tops open. Turn right side out and stuff lightly, so the limbs are quite floppy – don't stuff right to the top.

6 Draw three 1cm (½in) lines on the ends of the hands and sew to form fingers.

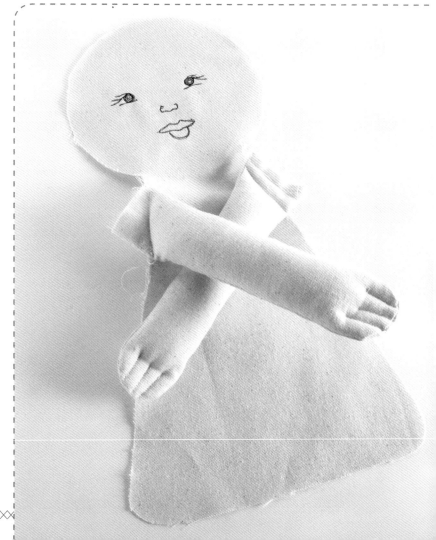

7 Mark the centre of the head, then draw the features just underneath this line. Free-motion embroider over the features, or hand embroider if you wish.

8 Tack/baste the arms to the sides of the body, 1cm (½in) from the neck and facing inwards.

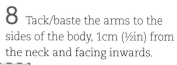

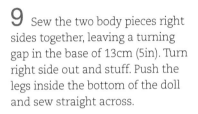

9 Sew the two body pieces right sides together, leaving a turning gap in the base of 13cm (5in). Turn right side out and stuff. Push the legs inside the bottom of the doll and sew straight across.

10 To make the dress, sew the short ends of the fabric right sides together to make a tube. Fold the bottom edge over twice and hem. Then loosen the tension on your machine, and sew two rows of long straight stitches, 1cm (½in) apart around the top edge. Pull the bottom thread to gather the fabric; place around the doll's chest and tighten. Tie the ends in a knot. Tie a length of ribbon around the top of the dress, and secure it in place with a little wet glue.

12 Cut the yarn off the ruler along one side, and drape over the top of the doll's head. Backstitch straight down the centre by hand, using a large needle and a piece of yarn to sew. I like to add a smear of fabric glue under the stitches to stop little fingers from pulling out the hair! Tie a length of ribbon around the head and add a bow. Sew a button to each shoe and one to the dress. Pop a little blusher on her cheeks.

13 Cut a piece of blackboard fabric approximately 2.5cm (1in) larger all round than the CD. Spread a little glue onto one side of the CD and wrap the fabric around it. Use the CD as a template to cut another piece of blackboard fabric; glue this to the other side of the CD. Fold the bias tape in half and press, then glue around the edge of the CD. Sew through the centre of the buttons, then glue in place to the edge of the blackboard. Pop a little glue onto the doll's hands, wrap around the board as if she is holding it, and hold in place until secure. Chalk on the number of the day as you count down!

11 To make the hair, wrap the yarn around a 15.25cm (6in) rectangular ruler – use a wider template if you want longer hair.

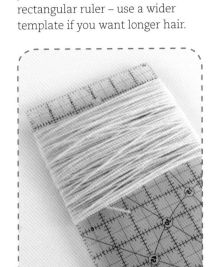

Snowman Calendar

This cheery character appears each year to say 'Christmas is coming!' to excited children and grown-ups alike. I've used white towelling fabric for his body; it does fray a lot so you may prefer to use white felt instead.

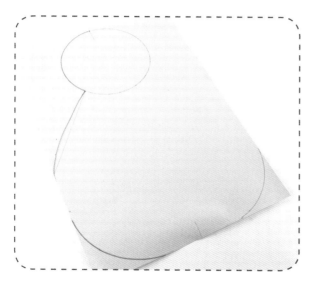

Finished size
45.75 x 71cm (18 x 28in)

What you need

102 x 66cm (40 x 26in) white towelling fabric

102 x 66cm (40 x 26in) foam stabiliser (you could use single-sided fusible foam stabiliser)

91.5 x 7.5cm (36 x 3in) fabric for the outer pockets: I found a fabric with snowmen printed on it and fussy cut the shapes, so I used 91.5 x 30.5cm (36 x 12in) of fabric instead

91.5 x 7.5cm (36 x 3in) plain fabric for the pocket linings

10cm (4in) square orange felt for the nose

Three large black buttons

7.5 x 89cm (3 x 35in) blue felt for the scarf

30.5 x 38cm (12 x 15in) red felt for the hat

Large white pompom

56 x 10cm (22 x 4in) white faux fur trim

Three red buttons

15.25 x 7.5cm (6 x 3in) green felt: I used two shades of green

250g (9oz) toy filler

Red and black embroidery thread and needle

Erasable ink pen

70 x 63.5cm (27½ x 25in) card

30.5cm (12in), 25.5cm (10in) and 10cm (4in) circle templates

Pink blusher

Temporary spray adhesive (not needed if you're using fusible foam stabiliser)

Numbers 1–12: I used foam numbers and strong fabric glue

Holly template, page 96

Optional: two twigs for arms, each measuring approximately 25.5cm (10in)

1 To make the template, mark the centre top and bottom of your card. Place the 25.5cm (10in) circle template at the top centre and draw around it. Use the 30.5cm (12in) circle template to curve the two bottom corners. To create the snowman's shoulders, mark 28cm (11in) up the left-hand edge of the card; draw a line from this mark to meet the circle. Curve this line slightly. Repeat on the other side.

2 Fold the card in half to make it symmetrical and cut out the snowman shape. Using this template, cut two pieces from towelling and two from foam stabiliser. Trim the stabiliser by 5mm (¼in) all the way round. Use spray adhesive to fix each piece of foam to the back of a piece of towelling.

Tip

If you make the pockets half
the size you could create a
twenty-four-pocket calendar.

3 Cut your 7.5cm (3in) pocket piece squares – twelve from patterned and twelve from lining fabric.

4 Sew each pair of patterned and plain squares right sides together, leaving a turning gap of about 2.5cm (1in) in the bottom. Snip across the corners.

5 Turn each pocket right side out and press. Don't worry if the pockets aren't all uniform in shape and size, this adds to the quirkiness of the calendar!

6 Arrange the pockets on top of a piece of towelling fabric. Don't place them too close to the edge of the snowman – as you don't want to trap them in the seam allowance – and allow room for the scarf. Pin in place, then sew around the three bottom sides of each pocket. Sew three black buttons to the tummy. Glue the numbers to the pockets.

7 Make 7.5cm (3in) cuts into each short end of the blue felt at 5mm (¼in) intervals to create a fringe.

8 To make the nose, use your 10cm (4in) circle template to make a curve in the felt from one corner to the opposite.

9 Sew the straight sides of the felt piece together to make a cone. Turn right side out and stuff with a little toy filler.

10 Hand sew the nose to the centre of the head. Draw a couple of curved lines for the eyes and mouth, then hand embroider over the top in black embroidery thread using backstitch. Add a little blusher to the cheeks by dotting it with your finger.

11 Place the two towelling pieces right sides together and sew all the way round, leave a turning gap of about 13cm (5in) in the base. Turn right side out. Push the toy filler into the snowman through the opening, just enough to give him a round belly and head. Hand sew the opening closed.

12 Cut the red felt into two triangles, 30.5cm (12in) tall and 25.5cm (10in) across. Sew together along the two long sides, then turn right side out.

13 Sew the strip of faux fur around the bottom of the hat, and the pompom to the point. Cut out your holly leaves using the template on page 96. Sew a running stitch in embroidery thread along the centre of each leaf. Hand sew these to one side of the hat, then add the three red buttons as berries.

14 Pop the hat on the snowman's head and secure with a few hand stitches. Hand sew the curtain ring to the back of the head to hang. If you decide to use twigs as arms, carefully unpick 1cm (½in) from each shoulder seam, insert the twigs, then hand sew either side to stop the seam from coming undone. Choose slim twigs so that they don't distort the shape of your snowman.

Quick Cones

These simple cones make perfect advent bunting – string them across a window, around a tree or even on a ladder!

Finished size

Each cone:
14 x 6.5cm (5½ x 2½in)

What you need

Fifty 15.25cm (6in) squares of fabric in an assortment of prints

12m (39½ft) of bakers' twine

Die-cut felt numbers, 1–25

Fabric glue

1 Take two contrasting fabric squares for each cone – one will form the outer, the other the lining. Place them right sides together and sew along two adjacent sides.

2 Pull the unsewn corners apart to form one large triangle. Sew along the open edge, leaving a turning gap in the lining side.

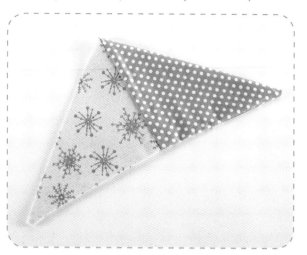

3 Turn right side out, sew the opening closed and press.

4 Push the lining inside the cone and press again, with the seam running centrally down the back.

5 Fold the point over to the front and glue in place.

6 Glue a felt number to the flap with fabric glue. Using a large needle, thread the bakers' twine through each side of the cone, leaving a length of slack for hanging. Knot the twine at each side of the cone before cutting. Repeat for the other twenty-four cones. Hang them up as you wish!

Calendar Cubes

Turn the cubes and match the numbers to mark the countdown to Christmas. This is a fun alternative to a wall-hanging calendar, and a great way to help the kids learn counting!

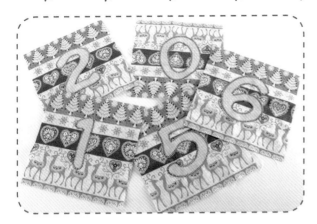

1 Fuse the adhesive to the wrong side of the number fabric, draw around the templates and cut the numbers out. Cube one will need numbers 1, 2, 3, 4, 5, and 6; cube two will need numbers 7, 8, 9, 0, 1 and 2. Iron a number to the centre of each square of fabric, then sew them in place. I've used a machine blanket stitch to edge my numbers.

2 Sew squares 1–4 into a strip, right sides together.

3 Sew the ends of the strip together to form a tube. Sew in the top and base pieces – numbers 5 and 6 – leaving a turning gap in one side of about 7.5cm (3in). Turn right side out and stuff with toy filler. Sew the opening closed by hand.

4 Repeat with the second cube.

Tip
As long as the fabric pieces are square they can be made in any size, so you could easily make a smaller version as a desktop calendar!

Advent Bunting

These fun pockets can be draped over a bed headboard, across a window or along shelves, and filled with fun treats for kids and grown-ups alike!

Finished size

Each pennant:
13 x 13cm (5 x 5in)

Length of bunting: about
4.5m (177in)

What you need

117 x 28cm (46 x 11in) of patterned fabric cut into twenty-five triangles measuring 14cm (5½in) across the top and 14cm (5½in) in height: you will be able to cut more triangles from your fabric if you use a non-directional print; allow more fabric if your print is directional: I used a combination of three prints

117 x 28cm (46 x 11in) of plain fabric cut into twenty-five triangles measuring 14cm (5½in) across the top and 14cm (5½in) in height: I used two colours

117 x 38cm (46 x 15in) plain fabric for the backing

Twenty-five buttons to fasten

127cm (50in) ribbon, 5mm (¼in) in width

Numbers 1–25: I used number buttons

15.25cm (6in) circle template

Marking pen

4.5m (177in) piping cord

1 Using one of your fabric triangles as a template, and using your plain backing fabric, draw around the two long sides, then use your circle template to make a dome shape on top. Cut fifty of these shapes.

Tip

For a different look, use brightly coloured ribbon instead of cord, and hold the pennants in place with decorated pegs!

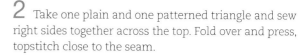

2 Take one plain and one patterned triangle and sew right sides together across the top. Fold over and press, topstitch close to the seam.

3 Place a domed piece down in front of you, with the right side facing up; put your sewn patterned piece patterned side down on top. Pin, then sew along one straight side. Tack/baste a 5cm (2in) length of looped ribbon, facing inwards, to the centre top.

4 Remove any pins. Place a second domed triangle on the top of the first, right sides facing, sandwiching the pocket in between. Sew all the way around, leaving a turning gap of about 5cm (2in) in the side you've already stitched. Snip off the point.

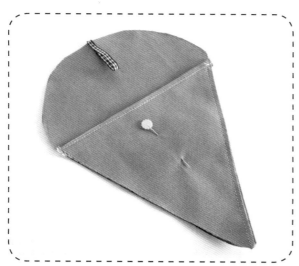

5 Turn right side out and hand sew the opening closed. Turn so that the patterned side of the pocket is on the outside and press.

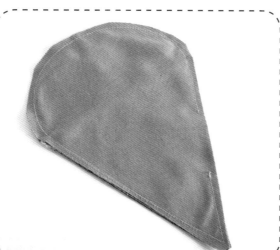

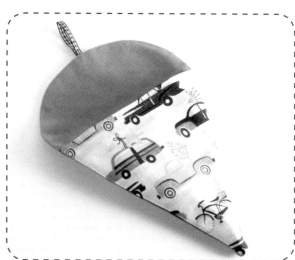

6 Fold the flap over and mark the position where the button will need to sit; hand sew the button on. Add the number to the flap. Repeat with the remaining twenty-four pockets. Thread the cord under the flaps and hang.

Tip
Use this technique without the numbers, pop a little Christmas pot pourri inside, and you'll have beautifully fragranced bunting.

Treat Bags

Fill a decorative bowl or basket with these treat-filled pouches, which make an interesting alternative to a wall-hanging calendar.

Finished size

Each bag:
7.5 x 14cm (3 x 5½in)

What you need

137cm (1½yd) of fabric cut into 100 rectangles of fabric, each measuring 9 x 15.25cm (3½ x 6in): I've used several co-ordinating prints

5m (197in) of string cut into twenty-five 20.5cm (8in) pieces

Safety pin or bodkin

Erasable ink pen

Ruler

Twenty-five tags

A felt pen

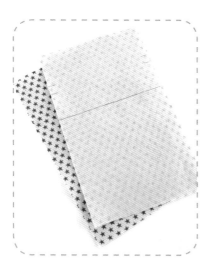

1 You will need two outer and two lining pieces of fabric for each bag. Measure and mark 6.5cm (2½in) down across the whole width of each lining piece using erasable pen. Then place edge marks 4cm (1½in) and 3cm (1¼in) down from the top of each lining piece.

2 To make the first bag, place each outer piece right sides together with a lining piece, and sew around the top, starting and stopping at the 6.5cm (2½in) markings, leaving a gap between the next two marks (these gaps will create a channel for the string to run through).

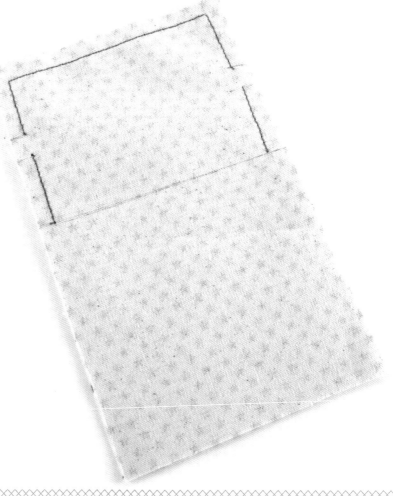

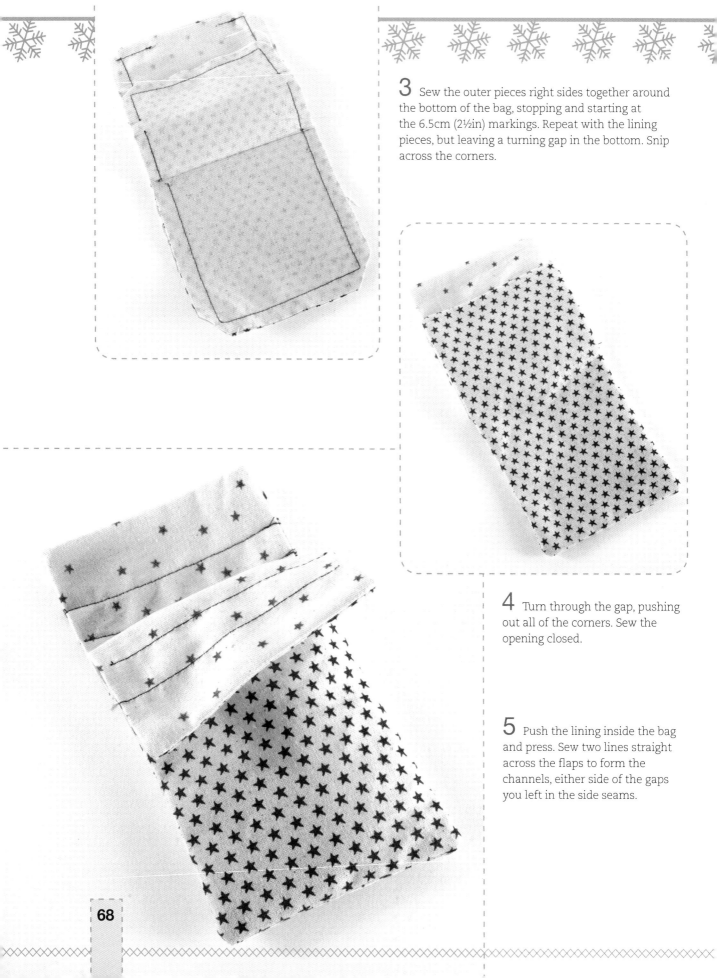

3 Sew the outer pieces right sides together around the bottom of the bag, stopping and starting at the 6.5cm (2½in) markings. Repeat with the lining pieces, but leaving a turning gap in the bottom. Snip across the corners.

4 Turn through the gap, pushing out all of the corners. Sew the opening closed.

5 Push the lining inside the bag and press. Sew two lines straight across the flaps to form the channels, either side of the gaps you left in the side seams.

6 Number your tags from 1 to 25 with a felt pen.

7 Knot a string piece onto the safety pin and thread through the channel. Fill with treats, then take both ends of the string through a tag and tie in a bow.

8 Repeat another twenty-four times!

Tip
You can make these bags in any size you like, so how about making matching Christmas gift bags!

Four-week Calendar

Turn the pages of this cool, contemporary calendar to count down the four weeks to Christmas!

Finished size

24 x 45.75cm (9½ x 18in)

What you need

For the pages:

Four pieces of fabric measuring 17.75 x 35.5cm (7 x 14in), 17.75 x 34.25cm (7 x 13½in), 17.75 x 33cm (7 x 13in) and 17.75 x 31.75cm (7 x 12½in)

Four pieces of wadding/batting measuring 17.75 x 17.75cm (7 x 7in), 17.75 x 17.25cm (7 x 6¾in), 17.75 x 16.5cm (7 x 6½in) and 17.75 x 16cm (7 x 6¼in)

Numbers 1–4 measuring approximately 10cm (4in) tall – I used plastic templates

Plain fabric for the numbers

Double-sided adhesive sheets

Scrap fabric for the appliqué shapes, buttons for the snowman's eyes and tree's baubles, bakers' twine and ribbon to decorate

Four buttons and 25.5cm (10in) bakers' twine to tie back the pages

For the backing:

Two pieces of fabric measuring 25.5 x 23cm (10 x 9in)

One piece of lining measuring 25.5 x 44.5cm (10 x 17½in)

Two pieces of wadding/batting measuring 25.5 x 23cm (10 x 9in)

Two pieces of 15.25cm (6in) long ribbon

28cm (11in) length of 5mm (¼in) wide dowelling to hang – I wrapped bakers' twine around mine

1 First make up the pages. Fold each fabric piece in half widthways, with wrong sides facing. When you lay them together you'll see that they vary slightly in size.

2 Iron the fusible sheet to the wrong side of the plain number fabric. Draw around your templates on the front of number fabric, then cut out numbers 1–4. Peel away the backing and iron the numbers onto the folded fabric pieces created in step 1, with the fold at the bottom. Number 1 should be on the largest piece, 4 on the smallest.

3 For the bauble appliqué pieces, cut two circles of fabric, one measuring 7.5cm (3in) and one measuring 9cm (3½in) across, with a little 'box' shape on top. The gift box is a 12.5cm (5in) square, the tree is a triangle measuring 12.5cm (5in) tall and 10cm (4in) across the base. Draw two overlapping circles, one measuring 7.5cm (3in) across and the other 6.5cm (2½in) – this makes the snowman. Use a 9cm (3½in) template for the star. Sew each shape right sides together with a scrap piece, make a cut in the scrap side and turn right side out. Press, then decorate with ribbons and trims.

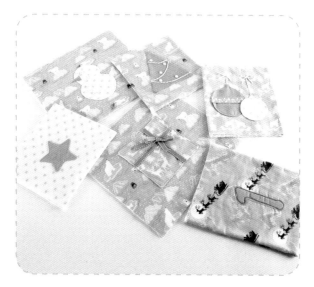

4 Open out the page pieces and place the wadding/batting behind the numbers. Free-motion embroider around the numbers. Sew the appliqué shapes to the opposite ends of the 2, 3 and 4 pieces; have them facing in the opposite direction. Place the remaining wadding/batting on the wrong sides of the backing fabric pieces, and sew the remaining appliqué shapes in the centre of each. Fold the number pieces in half right sides together. Sew them leaving the top open. Turn right side out and press. Add your buttons and bows.

5 Lay the pages on top of each other in order, with number 4 on top. Sandwich these centrally in between the two pieces of backing fabric and sew along the seam to join them all. Open out the calendar, fold the 15.25cm (6in) lengths of hanging ribbon in half and tack/baste, facing inwards to the top, 5cm (2in) from each side. Do the same with the 25.5cm (10in) length of twine, in the centre.

6 Sew this section right sides together with the lining, leaving a turning gap of about 10cm (4in) in one side. Snip across the corners. Turn right side out and press, then topstitch all the way round. Sew a small button to the top centre back of each page.

7 Push the dowelling through the ribbon loops, then tie on a 35.5cm (14in) length of twine for hanging.

Tip
Make up the calendar in a different fabric and you could be counting down to a wedding or special birthday!

Santa Express

How excited the kids are going to be when this treat-filled train appears! Start the numbers at twenty-four instead of one and you could make a 'sleeps-until-Christmas' calendar instead.

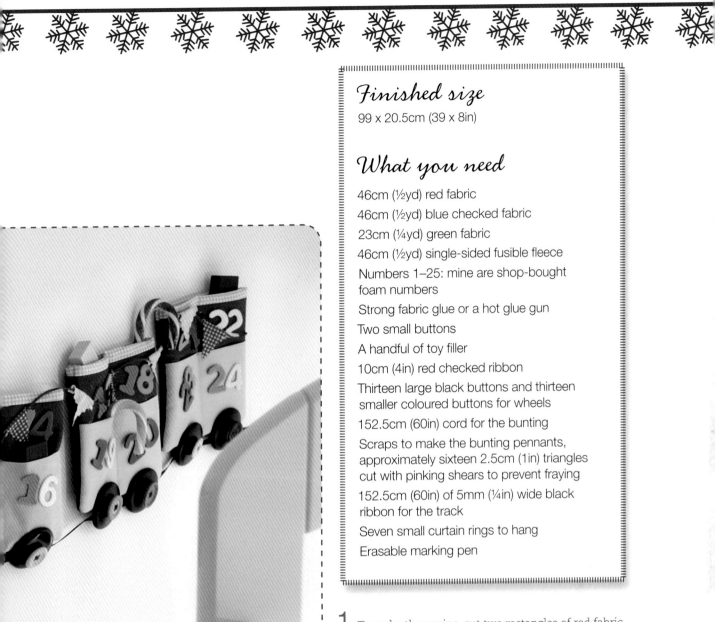

Finished size

99 x 20.5cm (39 x 8in)

What you need

46cm (½yd) red fabric

46cm (½yd) blue checked fabric

23cm (¼yd) green fabric

46cm (½yd) single-sided fusible fleece

Numbers 1–25: mine are shop-bought foam numbers

Strong fabric glue or a hot glue gun

Two small buttons

A handful of toy filler

10cm (4in) red checked ribbon

Thirteen large black buttons and thirteen smaller coloured buttons for wheels

152.5cm (60in) cord for the bunting

Scraps to make the bunting pennants, approximately sixteen 2.5cm (1in) triangles cut with pinking shears to prevent fraying

152.5cm (60in) of 5mm (¼in) wide black ribbon for the track

Seven small curtain rings to hang

Erasable marking pen

1 To make the engine, cut two rectangles of red fabric measuring 23 x 19cm (9 x 7½in). Cut away the top left-hand corner of each, 7.5cm (3in) down from the top and 10cm (4in) in from the side. Fuse the fleece to the wrong side of the front piece.

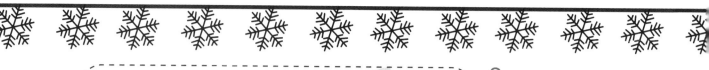

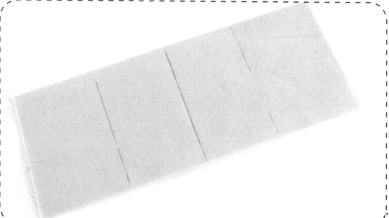

2 Cut a piece of green fabric measuring 23 x 18cm (9 x 7in), fold in half widthways and press. Mark the centre with a line, then 5.75cm (2¼in) either side to create four equal pockets.

3 Place this section over the padded side of the engine, tack/baste close to the edge on the bottom and side edges then sew along the three dividing lines to create the pockets.

4 To make the chimney, cut two triangles of blue checked fabric measuring 7.5cm (3in) across the bottom and 9cm (3½in) tall, then cut 2.5cm (1in) off the points. Sew right sides together around the three long sides, snip off the corners and turn right side out. Fill with a little toy filler. Wrap the red checked ribbon around the chimney and glue in place.

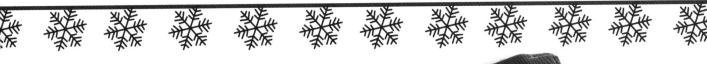

5 Tack/baste the chimney, facing inwards, to the top edge of the front of the train. Place the back piece of engine fabric on top, right sides facing, and sew all the way around, leave a turning gap in the roof of about 7.5cm (3in). Snip off the corners. Turn the engine right side out and press.

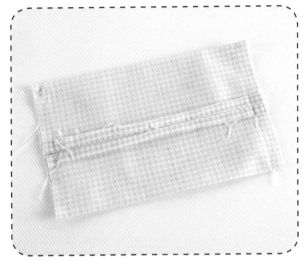

6 To make up the engine roof, cut a piece of blue checked fabric measuring 14 x 9cm (5½ x 3½in). Sew the two short ends right sides together to make a tube, leaving a gap of about 5cm (2in) in the middle of the stitches for turning. Position the seam in the centre, then sew over the ends.

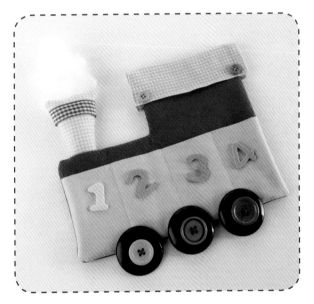

7 Snip the corners. Turn the roof right side out and press. Topstitch around the edge. Place the roof over the top of the train, with the open seam underneath. Sew across the top of the train.

8 Fold the roof over and secure it with two small buttons. (You could pop a little glue under the roof to hold it flat.) Glue a pinch of toy filler to the top of the chimney, and add numbers 1 to 4 to the pockets. Take a piece of embroidery thread and needle, and sew through the holes in the smaller coloured buttons. Glue or sew three large buttons to the bottom of the train for wheels, then the smaller buttons in the centre.

9 To make up the carriages, cut ten pieces of red fabric measuring 15.25 x 14cm (6 x 5½in) and fuse fleece to the back of each piece. Cut five pieces of green fabric measuring 15.25 x 18cm (6 x 7in), fold each in half widthways and press. Place each green piece over the bottom of five of the red pieces, with the fold at the top, and tack/baste together within the seam allowance – these are your front pocket pieces.

10 Cut ten pieces of blue checked fabric measuring 15.25cm (6in) square. Sew one blue piece to the top of each red piece (the five pocket front pieces and the five other red pieces), right sides together.

11 Place each front pocket piece right sides together with a plain piece – placing the blue checked pieces together and the red pieces together – and sew all the way round, leaving a turning gap of about 7.5cm (3in) in the blue checked side. Snip across the corners, then turn right side out. Sew the opening closed.

12 Push the lining inside the carriage. As the lining is a little larger, it will create a contrast trim around the top. Measure and mark the centre of the carriage and sew straight through all the layers to create four pockets. Repeat for the other four carriages.

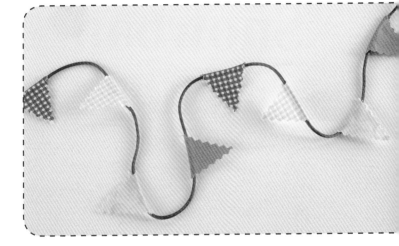

13 Glue on four numbers to the pockets. Add two large black and two smaller coloured buttons for wheels as in step 8.

14 Take your scrap fabric bunting pennants and glue them to the cord approximately 5cm (2in) apart. Wrap the top of the triangles over the cord as you glue.

15 Lay out the engine and carriages in a row on a flat surface. Position the bunting in a wavy line over all sections, then glue in place. Be careful not to glue over the pocket openings! Glue the strip of black ribbon behind the wheels to make a track. Hand sew two curtain rings to the top of the back of the engine, and one to the back of each carriage to hang.

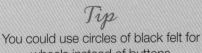

Tip
You could use circles of black felt for wheels instead of buttons.

Snowball Calendar

This calendar was inspired by silvery white snowballs tumbling down a hill on a crisp winter's morning – luckily though, you don't need to be out in the cold to enjoy these frosty treats!

Finished size

28 x 60cm (11 x 23½in)

What you need

One piece of background fabric measuring 30.5 x 51cm (12 x 20in)

One piece of contrast fabric for the sky measuring 30.5 x 23cm (12 x 9in)

One piece of lining measuring 30.5 x 61cm (12 x 24in) – I used the same fabric as my background

Five strips of pocket fabric, each measuring 30.5 x 11.5cm (12 x 4½in)

One piece of scrap fabric measuring 30.5 x 12.75cm (12 x 5in)

Fusible fleece measuring 30.5 x 76cm (12 x 30in)

Twenty-five 2.5cm (1in) buttons for the numbers

Twenty-five 5cm (2in) circles of fabric to cover the buttons

Number stamps and fabric ink

Three 2.5cm (1in) and three 1cm (½in) buttons for the snowballs

Scraps of white fabric to cover the snowball buttons

18cm (7in) ribbon for hanging

Erasable ink pen

30.5cm (12in) circle template

Strong wet fabric glue

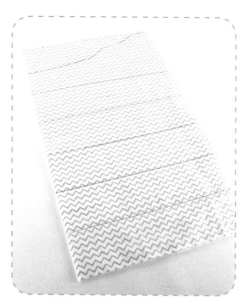

1 Fuse the fleece to the wrong side of the background fabric. Measure and mark a line across the width 7.5cm (3in) up from the bottom, then four more lines above this one, 7.5cm (3in) apart. Across the top of the fabric, draw a slightly wavy line to make a 'hill'.

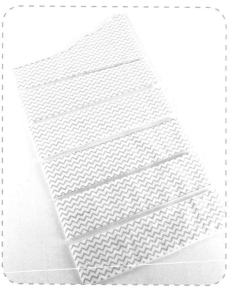

2 Cut across each drawn line, including the wavy line.

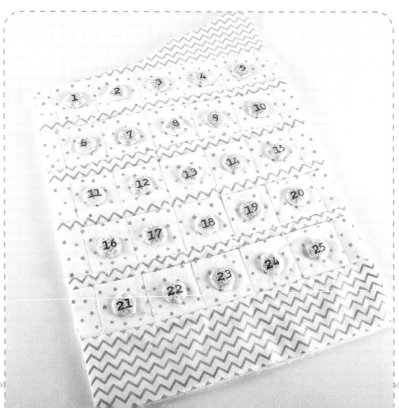

3 Fold each pocket strip in half lengthways and press. Measure and mark 2.5cm (1in) from each end, then at 5cm (2in) intervals across the pocket. This will create five pockets in each strip.

4 Sew each pocket strip in place between the cut strips of fabric, trapping the open edges of the folded pocket strips in the seams.

5 Stitch along the dividing lines to create pockets. Sew the wavy edge, right sides together with the scrap fabric, snip into the curves, turn right side out and press.

6 Cover each of the buttons with its circle of fabric and stamp on numbers 1–25. Add a button to each one of the pockets. As the buttons hang downwards when hand-sewn, I've glued them in place with strong fabric glue.

7 Take the lining and contrast fabric pieces and cut a curve across the top of each using your 30.5cm (12in) circle template.

8 Fuse fleece to the wrong side of the small curved piece. Place this behind the wavy edge and topstitch in place; trim away any bulky fleece. Cover your six snowball buttons and stitch in a random arrangement on top of the curved section.

9 Fold the ribbon in half and tack/baste to the centre top of the calendar, facing inwards. Place the buttoned side right sides together with the lining, trim away any excess fabric from the lining. Sew all the way around, leaving a turning gap of about 10cm (4in) in one side. Snip across the corners, turn right side out and press. Topstitch all the way around to complete.

Tip

If you have any leftover fabric, try knotting 2.5 x 12.5cm (1 x 5in) strips to a string of LED fairy lights to create a simple festive garland. Never leave lights on unattended.

Promise Tree

Fill this tree with festive promises and acts of good cheer! Each pocket has a tag that you can personalise with twenty-five promises leading up to Christmas day. These could be anything from 'I'll do the cooking today' to 'I'll tell you a funny story'. Use a different coloured pen for each member of the family so everyone can make promises throughout December!

Finished size
44.5 x 76.25cm (17½ x 30in)

What you need

1m (1yd) of festive background fabric

For the pockets, a 51cm (20in) square of contrasting fabric

51 x 71cm (20 x 28in) fusible fleece

Erasable ink pen

2.75m (9ft) of 2.5cm (1in) wide bias binding

Twenty-five card tags, measuring approximately 5 x 6.5cm (2 x 2½in)

One length of ribbon measuring 15.25cm (6in)

Twenty-five fusible pre-cut felt numbers

1 Cut two triangles of fabric measuring 48.25cm (19in) across the bottom and 71cm (28in) tall. Fuse the fleece to the wrong side of the front panel. Draw a line across, 2.5cm (1in) up from the bottom with your erasable ink pen, then six more lines above this at 7.5cm (3in) increments. Cut the contrasting pocket fabric into 10cm (4in) strips, fold in half lengthways and press. Lay them across the drawn lines and cut to size slightly wider than the tree.

2 Fold the bias tape in half lengthways and press. Fold it over the raw open edge of each pocket strip and sew. The edge with bias binding will be the top of the pocket.

3 Pin each pocket strip in place so that the bottoms of the pockets sit on the drawn lines; sew across the bottom. Remove the pins and trim the pockets to the shape of the tree.

4 Using your erasable ink pen, mark the dividing lines on the pockets, as shown right. You'll need six on the bottom row, five on the next, then four, another four, then three, two and finally one on the top. It's easier to place your labels in position and mark alongside them. Sew these dividing lines.

5 Fold the ribbon in half and tack/baste, facing inwards to the top of the tree. Place the backing fabric on top, right sides together, and sew all the way round, leaving a turning gap of 10cm (4in) in one side. Turn right side out and press. Topstitch all the way round.

6 Write out your promises!

7 Fuse the numbers to the pockets, then pop in your promises.

Canine Calendar

There's no need to leave your faithful friend out of the festive fun this year – but do make sure you hang their calendar out of reach so that the biscuits aren't all eaten on the first day!

Finished size

79 x 28cm (31 x 11in)

What you need

51 x 25.5cm (20 x 10in) outer coat fabric
51 x 25.5cm (20 x 10in) coat lining fabric
84 x 45.75cm (33 x 18in) wadding/batting
84 x 45.75cm (33 x 18in) dog body fabric
25.5 x 20.5cm (10 x 8in) ear fabric
10cm (4in) circle template
Erasable ink pen
152.5cm (60in) of 2.5cm (1in) wide bias binding
Handful of toy filler
Numbers 1–24: I've used shop-bought wooden numbers
61cm (24in) length of 1cm (½in) wooden dowelling
432cm (170in) string
Fabric glue
Twenty-four 5cm (2in) long bone-shaped biscuits
Templates, page 95

1 Mark on your body fabric a rectangle measuring 49.5 x 18cm (19½ x 7in), but don't cut this out yet. Place your dog head template at the top of one end and the tail at the top of the other end; draw around these shapes onto the fabric. Round off the bottom two corners of the rectangle with your circle template. You'll have a long, legless dog shape; cut out two pieces.

2 Cut out four foot pieces using your template. Sew right sides together in pairs, leaving the top open. Snip into the curves, turn right side out and stuff with a little toy filler.

3 Cut a piece of wadding/batting to the same shape as the body. Fuse it to the wrong side of the front of the dog with spray adhesive if you wish. Tack/baste the feet, facing upwards, to the tummy, 5cm (2in) from each side.

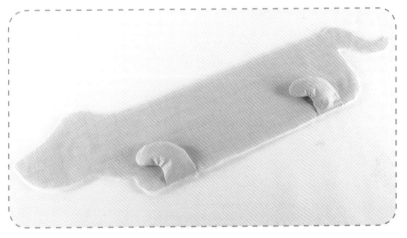

4 Pin the two body pieces right sides together and sew all the way round, leaving a turning gap of about 10cm (4in) across the dog's back. Remove the pins and turn right side out. Hand sew the opening closed.

5 Cut out two ear pieces using your template. Sew right sides together, leaving the top open. Snip around the curves, then turn right side out and press, with the open top tucked inwards.

6 Pleat the top of the ear and sew to the dog's head, 2.5cm (1in) from the centre top. Hand sew a French knot as an eye.

7 To make the coat, draw a 2.5cm (1in) grid all over the outer fabric with an erasable ink pen. Place the lining wrong sides together with the outer fabric, with the wadding/batting sandwiched in between, then sew over each line to quilt. Trim the edges if necessary, then use your circle template to curve the bottom two corners, as shown.

8 Apply bias binding all around the coat; fold over the first end of the tape, then overlap the opposite end when they meet.

9 To mitre the corners, stop sewing 5mm (¼in) before the corner, keep the needle in the fabric but lift the presser foot, then fold the tape to create a neat triangle. Line up the edges of the tape and coat and continue sewing along the next edge (see page 14).

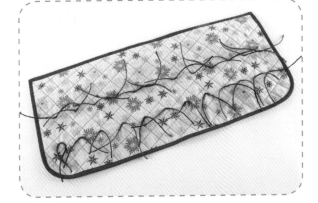

10 Wrap the binding around the edge of the coat and sew, either by hand from the back of the coat or by machine from the front.

11 Draw two lines across the coat with an erasable ink pen, 11.5cm (4½in) and 16.5cm (6½in) from the top. Make twelve marks across each line, 4cm (1½in) apart. Cut twenty-four 15.25cm (6in) lengths of string, and hand sew one over each of these marks.

12 Place the coat over the dog, wrapping the top of the coat over the dog's back by about 4cm (1½in). Pin, then sew to the back of the dog across the top of the bias binding.

13 Fold the coat back over the dog. Tie a biscuit to each piece of string, then trim the string if necessary. Glue numbers 1–12 across the top of the first row, and numbers 13–24 underneath the second row. Pop a little glue onto the back of the coat to hold it in place.

14 Thread the dowelling through the back of the coat and tie the remaining string to each end to hang.

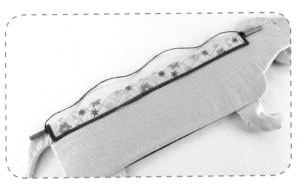

Tip
You could use a button for the eye, and why not make your pooch a collar?

Hanging Mittens

These simple little mittens would make a lovely project for crafty kids during the festive season. I've sewn around the mittens with a machine, but they could just as easily be sewn by hand.

Finished size

Each mitten: 10 x 13cm (4 x 5in)

What you need

Twenty-five 23cm (9in) felt squares in assorted colours

Embroidery thread and needle

Erasable marking pen

Twenty-five small wooden craft pegs

230cm (90½in) of 1cm (½in) wide ribbon to hang

Fabric glue

Mitten template, page 96

1 Cut out fifty mitten shapes using the template on page 96. Use pinking shears to cut across the top to give a 'furry' effect. Taking twenty-five of the mittens, draw on numbers 1–25 with your erasable ink pen.

2 Hand sew over the numbers with a chain stitch in embroidery thread.

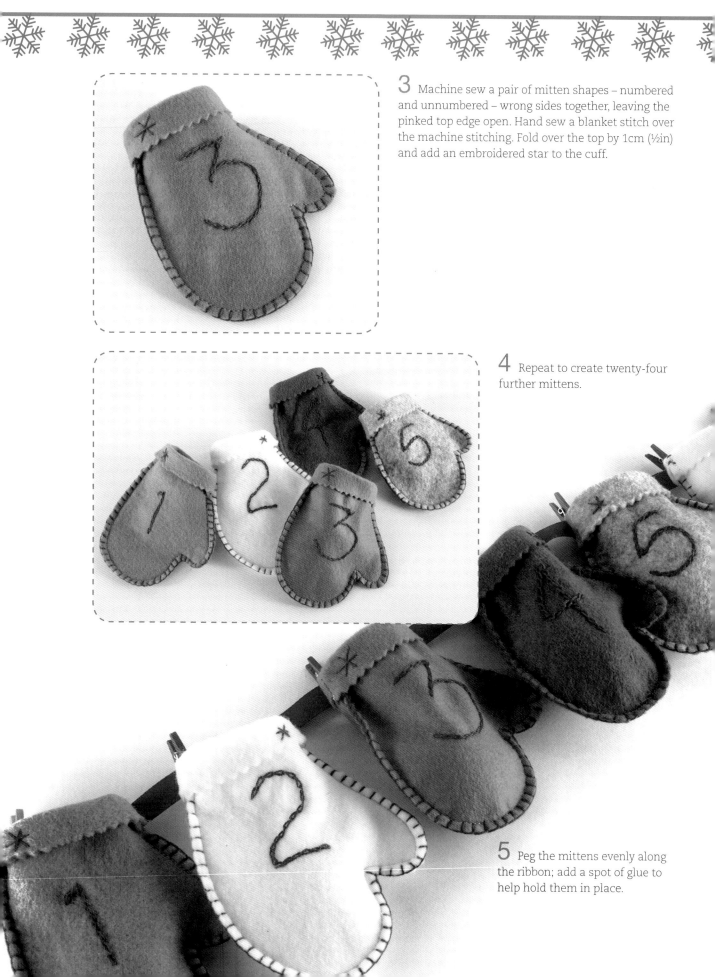

3 Machine sew a pair of mitten shapes – numbered and unnumbered – wrong sides together, leaving the pinked top edge open. Hand sew a blanket stitch over the machine stitching. Fold over the top by 1cm (½in) and add an embroidered star to the cuff.

4 Repeat to create twenty-four further mittens.

5 Peg the mittens evenly along the ribbon; add a spot of glue to help hold them in place.

Templates

All the templates are given at actual size.
Simply trace them off and cut them out.

Dog's head, tail, leg and ear for the Canine Calendar, see pages 88–91

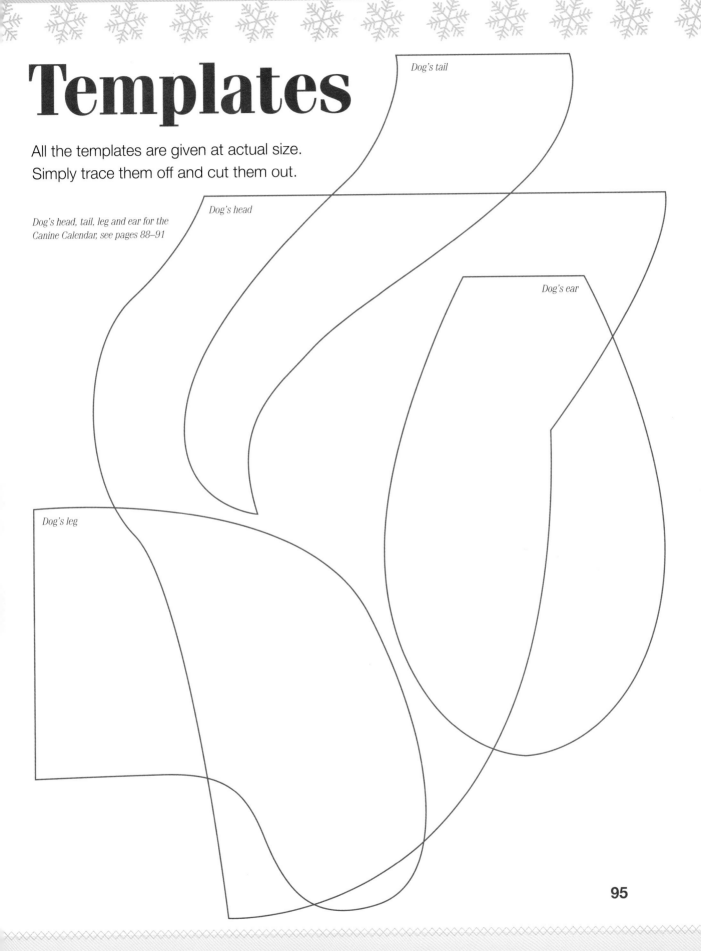

Dog's tail

Dog's head

Dog's ear

Dog's leg

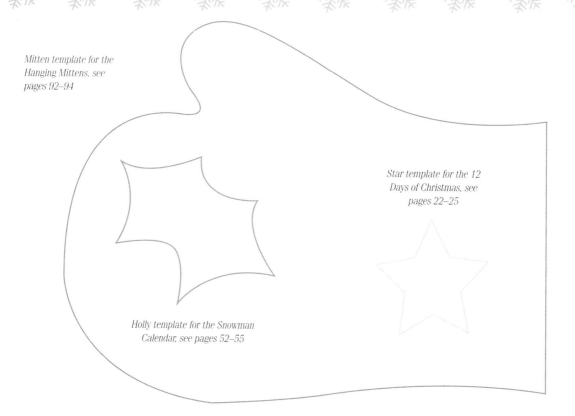

Mitten template for the Hanging Mittens, see pages 92–94

Star template for the 12 Days of Christmas, see pages 22–25

Holly template for the Snowman Calendar, see pages 52–55

Index